The Stations of the Cross for Alcoholics

by Paul Sofranko

photography by Rose Sofranko

Copyright 2011 Paul Sofranko and Rose Sofranko

Table of Contents

Preface

Welcome to this devotional booklet "The Stations of the Cross for Alcoholics."

The Stations are an ancient devotion in the Catholic Faith, usually said in Catholic parishes during Lent. Individuals for their own spiritual development often say them throughout the year.

The first page of each Station is a brief prayer (familiar to Catholics who practice the Stations in Lent) followed by a brief meditation on that Station's theme.

The photographs are from Sts. Peter and Paul Catholic Church in Hamburg, NY, USA, and were taken by my wife, Rose Sofranko. She also has a website at www.Artist4God.net.

I hope they help sort out the pain and suffering of alcoholism, and bring some help and relief.

This book is merely intended for spiritual growth and progress, it promises nothing more.

Thank you, and my prayers are with you on your sober journey.   Paul

The First Station: Jesus is Condemned to Death

We adore You, O Christ and We Praise You.

Because by Your Holy Cross You have redeemed the World

In this First Station of the Cross, we see how Jesus stood before His human judge and humbly allowed judgment to be passed upon Him. We meditate on how we ourselves have dealt with the judgments of others on our alcoholic past.

Jesus is brought before Pontius Pilate, the Roman governor of Israel. He has been accused of crimes He did not commit. He also offers no defense to his accusers. Jesus was innocent of the things He was charged with. We, however, were guilty of the things that we did while we were drinking and drugging. People had right reason to condemn us for our actions. We hurt others, disappointed many, and in general behaved irresponsibly. All to varying degrees, of course, but all of us had caused pain in other people.

Have we borne our offenses with the same humility as did Jesus? He had every right and justification, in light of human reason, to fight back against His accusers. But He took it silently, offering no defense. He turned the other cheek, if you will. How have we reacted to the pain and resentment sent our way by the people we had hurt? We deserve the lack of trust that others have shown us, and the cold treatment that takes a long time to thaw. But did He deserve His agony?

We had committed wrongs against others during our drinking periods. We have no reason now to make excuses or to offer up any defense for our actions. We must seek to make amends when possible and appropriate. But to bristle with annoyance, or to blame it on the addiction and excusing it that way is not the way to maintain sobriety.

Everyone dies a little death when confronted with evidence of his or her own wrongdoing. It is our conscience reacting to our less-than-exemplary behavior. Our addiction was the root cause of the behavior, but we cooperated with it. That part of ourselves that carried the behavior forward is purged. Our remorse and repentance helps to get rid of that character defect. We are different than before. Better, if we amend the relationships and ask what else can be done to repair it?

In this First Station of the Cross, an innocent Man is condemned to death. In our own First Station of the Cross, the person condemned to death is our addictive self. Even if we had been clean and sober for years, meditating on this can help keep that person dead.

5

<u>The Second Station: Jesus Takes up His Cross</u>

We adore You, O Christ and We Praise You.

Because by Your Holy Cross You have redeemed the World

In this Second Station of the Cross, we see how Jesus accepts and takes

up His Cross. We meditate on how well we, as His disciples, have

accepted our own Crosses.

Jesus takes up His cross after having been condemned by Pilate, and is led along the way of suffering to His eventual execution.

As Christians we are followers of Christ. We are called to be like Him. We are called to live like Him, and if called, die like Him.

As Christians we accept the crosses that come into our daily lives. Whether they are major life-threatening situations and other survival issues, or just merely little things that are sometimes tough to handle, we cannot reject and run away from them.

Christianity, especially Catholic Christianity, finds value in suffering. Suffering teaches us about ourselves and helps us to learn what is truly worthwhile in life. Without suffering, how can we appreciate joy?

It helps us to grow closer to God, for as His Son Jesus suffered for who He was, so we must suffer for being His followers. It isn't easy being a Christian in a world that is opposed to the message of the Gospel.

As recovering alcoholics and addicts, we had plenty of crosses to bear. Most people would call them "normal life", as quite often we found things difficult that others took in stride. As a result of our inability or refusal to deal with them, we drank or drugged.

Now we have new crosses to bear, we need to rebuild our lives and learn how to react to things without the crutch of alcohol. No longer is drinking a line of defense or an escape route. Now we have to face our troubles steadfastly and suffer through them.

Each of us has one of more crosses to bear. Many of us do it alone, silently enduring whatever befalls us, toiling and suffering without comfort, occupying a lonely outpost of grief or pain. Whether it is pain caused by other people, through their meanness and cruelty, or our own self-inflicted wounds, many of us know the Cross. Sometimes we grow through that suffering and become better for it.

Jesus took up His cross. In your Second Station of the Cross, how do you handle yours?

9

The Third Station: Jesus Falls the First Time

We adore You, O Christ and We Praise You.

Because by Your Holy Cross You have redeemed the World

In this Third Station of the Cross, we see how Jesus fell under the burden He was carrying. We meditate on our own journey of sobriety and our own stumbles and falls.

The path of sobriety is a lifelong one. It is not easy. We can be said to be like newborns, crawling along at first before learning enough about our newfound skills to practice walking. It is a path of suffering that does not make establishing a new life and learning its new rules very easy.

There are many struggles along that path. Too often the temptation to surrender to a drink is great.

"What would just one hurt? I know enough by now to just put the bottle away after one or maybe two. I can handle it. I'm stronger and better now, not as "powerless" over it as I was before."

But just one can hurt plenty. In addition to the guilt and remorse over the failure is also the blow to a fragile self-esteem that now is prone to believing that sobriety is basically impossible.

With tools that are poorly used or not fully understood, the newly clean and sober person falls. A relapse occurs.

Crushed by the weight of the suffering, crushed by the

enormity of the task, crushed by a promise that seems hard to achieve, a person falls. And crushed by the guilt over the failure to remain clean and sober, the temptation to remain fallen looms.

But driven by a purpose that outweighs the short-term pain, the person finds a moral resolve and gets up and continues along the path they have chosen. The cross of establishing a sober life is picked up and again the struggle begins.

As Jesus fell, bearing the weight of His cross, so might you fall (or have fallen). Do not let a relapse defeat you. Whether the relapse happened a long time ago and you are still ashamed of being human, or it just happened yesterday, learn from your mistakes and shortcomings.

When you experience your Third Station, or feel that you might be entering it, reach out to Jesus for help. He might be in the form of other people waiting and willing to assist you.

And if you still fall, you have fallen. Get back up. Learn, and resume your path of sobriety.

13

The Fourth Station: Jesus Meets Mary, His Mother

We adore You, O Christ and We Praise You.

Because by Your Holy Cross You have redeemed the World

In the Fourth Station of the Cross we see Jesus meet His Mother, who

was powerless to help Him. We meditate on how well we have come to

the aid of others we have met along the road of sobriety.

15

On the path of pain and suffering where the addictive self is going to die, the person encounters love.

It might be the addict's own mother, or some other nurturing figure. Perhaps it is when the alcoholic is reaching out for help and someone reaches back. It might be a 12 Step group.

Consolation and comfort are offered. A helping hand and guidance is provided. Or maybe just love and acceptance is freely given, without any consideration of being repaid.

Nevertheless, the person suffering experiences the first kindness directed towards them. The strength to continue is increased, if only by just enough.

The darkness that embraced the suffering alcoholic brightens ever so slightly. It is oftentimes difficult to see, when darkness is all about you, when people miss you or are concerned about your situation. Consumed by self-pity, the sufferer cannot imagine why anyone would reach out a helping hand to them. This is why we must not ever shut our eyes to those around us still in pain from their addictions.

One never knows when a hand reaching out to help will appear like a bright beam of sunlight in a blackened room.

Have you experienced your Fourth Station? While you trudged your way of the Cross, how often had you experienced such a kindness? Didn't it help? If you have traveled far enough along to remember this from your early sobriety, have you extended your hand to others in need?

Have you met someone in this way?

The Fifth Station: Simon of Cyrene Helps Jesus Carry His Cross

We adore You, O Christ and We Praise You.

Because by Your Holy Cross You have redeemed the World

In this Fifth Station of the Cross we see how Simon of Cyrene was

pressed into service to carry Christ's Cross when He was too weary.

We meditate on how often we have come to the aid of someone who was

seemingly on the verge of going no further on their road.

You're at a 12 Step meeting because it's your habit to do so. You see someone arrive. Some members look pitiably at him, whom you recognize as the newcomer who showed up two weeks straight smelling of alcohol. You and the others ignore him; perhaps he'll just leave.

No, the newcomer heads for the coffee machine and tries to fill a cup. Some coffee spills out as he lifts it up, and by the time the cup arrives at his lips about half has spilled out onto the floor.

You and your companions exchange cynical looks. The shaky newcomer keeps to the rear of the room hoping to hide, but accidentally kicks over a metal folding chair. All heads swivel back and witness that his stumbling finishes off the rest of his coffee. He sits down in a slump, head down, and an icon-image of defeat.

You suddenly feel something welling up inside you. It is as if a hand is rising up from within and is shaking loose some bits of conscience. You might have to do something that you don't want to do.

You try and resist. He wouldn't listen. I don't have the

time. I just show up here for coffee and conversation and maybe to hear what the old-timers say. It's a wasted effort, I've tried to help the relapse poster-children before, and it's never worked, so why now?

It is of no use. That something from within you becomes too strong and you get up, despite the start of the meeting. You avoid people's gaze as you make your way to the back.

You lean forward, touch him by the arm and whisper to the person, "Hey, my name is Simon, and I'm an alcoholic," you pause, "like you." The person looks up, the barest glimmer of hope shows in his eyes.

You continue, "We'll sit together, you and me." You recall that no one spoke to him after the previous two meetings. Last week he left immediately after it. "Afterwards we'll go outside and chat. Sound OK?"

The person rises up from his slump, as if a cross was lifted from his shoulders. Hope renewed, just from someone reaching out, however unwillingly at first in his Fifth Station.

The Sixth Station: Veronica Wipes the Face of Jesus

We adore You, O Christ and We Praise You.

Because by Your Holy Cross You have redeemed the World

In this Sixth Station of the Cross we see how Veronica was given the gift

of Christ's "true image." We meditate on how we must recover our

true selves, and see our true image as being made in the image and

likeness of God.

Jesus stops along the way to His Crucifixion and receives a moment's kindness by a woman, Veronica. She wipes His blood-and spit-splattered face with a cloth, and as one of His last miracles He leaves an imprint of His face on it. His image.

What about "true image" as it relates to you? When you were drinking, was that the real you? No. Yet some of us started drinking because we didn't feel "real". We didn't connect with others very well; we were "outsiders." When we drank it was as if a veil was drawn away from our eyes and we suddenly "understood" and "fit in."

Drinking was a liberation, and in our minds we rewrote the day's events - and always to our satisfaction. Wrongs were righted and slurs responded to with great wit. But that wasn't really who we were.

Recovery is about finding our true self, the "true image" of what God meant for us to be. In our recovery, we strip away all of our character defects and misdirected instincts, and learn to build a new life and embark upon the mission that God placed us on Earth for.

We were born for a reason; we were not put upon the Earth to be drunken fools. Revisit this Sixth Station often in your journey.

Of the Stations, this is the one that most likely did not occur (not all are Scriptural, but reason holds that all probably happened). The usual reason for the idea that this event never happened is the name "Veronica", which is a combination of the Latin and Greek words for "true image".

I think the legend of Veronica did happen, but the lady's name was never known, because I like to think that she escaped quickly from the street so the Romans wouldn't grab her. And therefore the small community of Jesus' followers made up a nice name for her.

The Seventh Station: Jesus Falls the Second Time

We adore You, O Christ and We Praise You.

Because by Your Holy Cross You have redeemed the World

In this Seventh Station, we see Jesus fall a second time.

We meditate on our heavy burdens and how we sometimes do not

possess the fortitude needed to maintain our path of sobriety.

As if we needed more proof that we are human, we find ourselves collapsing again under the weight of our trials and sufferings. Courage and fortitude develop with each failure and subsequent rising up. As Jesus fell a second time because of His human weakness under the strain of His Way of the Cross, so, too, might we also suffer another fall along our own path of suffering.

As was mentioned earlier, the way of early sobriety isn't an easy one. There are too many challenges and pitfalls as one learns how to react in a sober manner to the hardships of daily living. But what if your second fall comes much later? How many times in a 12-Step meeting have you heard that so-and-so had a relapse, and people were in amazement because he had 20 years of sobriety? What happened?

Being human is what happened. No one's sobriety is so assured that after achieving some success with it they are guaranteed that the road they are trudging is smooth from then on until death. Everyone is one drink away from a fall.

Keep this in mind when your guard seems too secure, when you are convinced that you have beaten alcoholism. It is often said in 12 Step meetings that the person with the longest sobriety is the one who woke up earliest that day.

Never take your sobriety for granted. And never assume that it is cumulative, that you build strength over time. In a way the longer you are sober the better, for you have probably weathered many a storm. But there is always a chance that overconfidence or a lapse of vigilance can derail you. You may not have visited your Seventh Station, yet.

The Eighth Station: Jesus Meets the Women of Jerusalem

We adore You, O Christ and We Praise You.

Because by Your Holy Cross You have redeemed the World

In this Eighth Station, we see the Women of Jerusalem mourn for Jesus.

We meditate on the sympathy and sorrow that others have for us that

may be misplaced.

I read something once, years ago, in a Lenten devotional meditation about this. I do not remember where as I no longer have the book. The writer had stated that back in the day of Roman crucifixions, Jewish women had the custom of going to the road leading to the crucifixion site and habitually mourned the condemned.

If I recall correctly, the women would do this despite that fact that they rarely knew the condemned. I think it was said that they did it because usually the condemned had no one to mourn for them and this was a way to expiate their own sins (but I may be wrong about that last part.)

If indeed that is the case then this is rather symbolic for the recovering alcoholic. The person in recovery trudges along a difficult path. There are people who mean well and see the person suffer. They react strongly to the person's attempt at sobriety. Whether they themselves are drinking and don't wish to be reminded of the troubles associated with it, or they have a misplaced sense of compassion and hate to see the person suffer, they don't like what they see.

Jesus' speech to the women of Jerusalem in the Gospel of Luke reminds us that He had little interest in their concern for Him. They were to weep for themselves because Jesus foresaw the fall of Jerusalem decades hence. So to, does the alcoholic desire not the pity or sympathy of misplaced or misguided people. A path of sobriety has been chosen, it must be finished and the concern of others should be spent properly. Be mindful when experiencing your Eighth Station.

The Ninth Station: Jesus Falls the Third Time

We adore You, O Christ and We Praise You.

Because by Your Holy Cross You have redeemed the World

In this Ninth Station Jesus falls for the third time under the pain of the

Cross's weight, and the torturous journey He has endured on the way

to His Crucifixion. We meditate on the sometimes overwhelming nature

of suffering and how insurmountable problems sometimes seem.

Somewhere down the path of sobriety the alcoholic has become overwhelmed by events. Something serious and very bad has happened in life. It might be the loss of a job, or a spouse has died. It could be serious health issues. Any of these, perhaps combined with a few others about the same time, and the struggle and stress to survive becomes to great to bear. I know people who have experienced multiple grave trials and have survived. Others have not.

The alcoholic is miserable and is consumed by despair. The oppressive weight of reality hits and there is another relapse.

Will the pain ever end? Will there ever be freedom?

In the despair there is surrender. Not necessarily the kind spoken of in the 12 Steps, but of another. There is a surrender of all the pain and troubles and all emotional connections to these.

This is surrendering to the will of God in another way. It makes it a little more specific for the confused alcoholic. It narrows it down to specifics, namely that of the pain and all other emotional connections to the addictive past and current troubled present, and places them in the will of God.

In this Ninth Station, the third fall of the alcoholic along their way, the person finds the strength to get up yet again.

There will be no final victory of the addiction over me! I will rise up!

And so once again the alcoholic rises up out of misery.

From somewhere within, the alcoholic has the conviction to never surrender. Every time before this when they have arisen from the ashes of a relapse, they have gotten a glimpse of the freedom of sobriety. They have the taste of it, and want it again.

37

<u>The Tenth Station: Jesus is Stripped of His Clothes</u>

We adore You, O Christ and We Praise You.

Because by Your Holy Cross You have redeemed the World

In this Tenth Station of the Cross, we see Jesus being stripped of His

garments. We meditate upon how we pray to have our external false

selves, our character defects stripped from us.

The suffering alcoholic becomes teachable. After the path of pain and agony that has been experienced since stopping drinking, there is now a willingness to be stripped of past conditioned behavior and learn a new set of rules. The alcoholic learns how to react to things in a sober manner. The suffering has reached a point where the façade is removed: the false exterior previously shown to others and through which he had interacted with reality.

The character defects are being removed.

Reality is now accepted for what it is and life is adjusted to that reality and serenity is the result.

Pray that your "clothing" be stripped off of you and that you are able to "put on Christ", the visible actions that indicate to others that you are apart from the world, that you are now living out your vocation of being God's adopted child.

For you are an adopted child of God. He is your Father and Jesus is your Brother and the Holy Spirit is your Guide and Teacher.

In the poisoning of our self-esteem that alcoholism does to us, it is often difficult, perhaps impossible to feel that we are in these relationships with the Trinity. That is one of the lies that we bought into. That we are not worth it and so only by means of drinking and drugging can we "feel better" about ourselves. It is as if the fantasies we concoct are better than our true selves.

But this is so not the case. Our true self that becomes revealed when the garbage is stripped away is far better. That is the creation we are supposed to be. The Author of all Creation designed us, just as He did the Universe and all the truth and Beauty contained within. He took all of Eternity to contemplate, plan and start Creation, and our part within it is just as important as the creation of any galaxy.

Through prayer and meditation you can dwell in the Father, Son and Holy Spirit and They in you, and this indwelling will grow. In your Tenth Station you will experience a healing of your past.

The Eleventh Station: Jesus is Nailed to the Cross

We adore You, O Christ and We Praise You.

Because by Your Holy Cross You have redeemed the World

In this Eleventh Station we see Jesus being nailed to the Cross. We meditate on our sins committed during our alcoholism, and we nail them to the Cross.

The Cross is the symbol of death, but in the case of Jesus it represents life. This is the "contradiction of the Cross", that a symbol of death represents life to all who believe.

Jesus died for our sins. We had put Him to death, from Adam's Original Sin, thus the need for Jesus to redeem us, from our own sins through today. He suffered for all of us.

Nail them to the Cross. Confess your sins to a priest and then nail the memory of the event to the Cross. Jesus died so that sin can be washed away, no matter how great or small. Several years ago I attended a Daily Mass and the little old priest gave a sermon in which he mentioned what Jesus might say to you about your sinning and confessing. It is helpful to remember this when you have trouble moving past your actions. The priest said that Jesus might say: "I died for you, and have forgiven and forgotten all your sins."

Nail your past misdeeds to the Cross in your Eleventh Station. Confess first and do penance, then watch the past die and become just a "learning experience." For what is experience than what we learned from past mistakes, even sinful ones?

Try and become emotionally disconnected from your past misdeeds. They are there, in the past. That is where they belong. You do not need to bring them into the present with you.

Learn from them so that they do not happen again. Otherwise, let them die on the Cross.

The Cross is a contradiction for people. A symbol of death becomes a symbol for life. The new life that awaits.

The Twelfth Station: Jesus Dies on the Cross

We adore You, O Christ and We Praise You.

Because by Your Holy Cross You have redeemed the World

In this Twelfth Station, Jesus dies upon the Cross. So, too, do our

addictive, alcoholic selves die and are consigned to the past.

The long struggle is over. The old addictive self is weakening and is losing its grip on the person.

The alcoholic has learned the skills of sobriety, has learned how to not react to things with fear and immediately dive for the security of a bottle. Anxiety is met with faith. The old ways are now becoming a distant memory. Painful memories, yes, but the pain is no longer in control. It flavors the memory as a motivator. "If I do this, then that will occur."

The practicing alcoholic dies in their own Twelfth Station, never to be resurrected for as long as the sober person remains vigilant and secure in the Faith.

The alcoholic has a deeper faith in God through the Catholic Church. It is now recognized as the primary source of all the spiritual healing for the alcoholic, for the Sacraments of healing exist with the Church. Confession and Holy Communion are frequently sought.

Strengthened by these Sacraments, the newly sober continues to turn their new life and will over to God, and to trust in His Mercy and Providence.

The Divine Healer has been met and embraced, and the alcoholic has taken Him into their home.

A new life of sobriety is now enjoyed.

The past is put to rest, inasmuch as it will no longer haunt the present. It serves as a memory, and a reminder.

The Thirteenth Station: Jesus' Body is Removed From the Cross

We adore You, O Christ and We Praise You.

Because by Your Holy Cross You have redeemed the World

In this Thirteenth Station, Jesus' Body is removed from the Cross. We meditate on preparing to bury the old alcoholic life.

51

The past needs to be dealt with. It cannot be dragged around like an anchor, nor can it take up residence in your life like an unwanted guest. To allow it to do so would be to prevent any further spiritual growth and development.

You cannot move forward while sometimes glancing back. Living in the past prevents you growing in the present.

Take the memories of your sinful past and remove then from the cross. Try, through prayer and meditation, to remove the emotional parts of the past from the events themselves.

Prepare to bury these things. You nailed them to the Cross of Christ to offer them up in union with His suffering and death. They are gone now. Jesus has healed you. The burial does not mean repressing; it means that you must leave them in the past where they belong. Memories of the events of the past should be sufficient in and of themselves to serve as a reminder of a life no longer worth living. As was mentioned in the Twelfth Station, the memories should serve as a motivator for

continued sobriety. There is no need for the emotions that will just tie you to living in that past.

The longer that you remain emotionally connected to the events of the past, and an alcoholic life no longer lived, the more difficult it will be for you to maintain a hold on your present and future sobriety.

The alcoholic has been nailed to the Cross. Now bury that person in your Thirteenth Station.

53

The Fourteenth Station: Jesus is Buried

We adore You, O Christ and We Praise You.

Because by Your Holy Cross You have redeemed the World

In this Fourteenth Station, we see Jesus is buried. And so too, do we meditate on the release we feel when we "bury" our alcoholic past.

And so we bury our past where it belongs, in the past and use its memories-minus-the-emotions as a motivator to maintain our sobriety. We then can move forward.

We bid farewell to our alcoholic self, it is still a part of us although no longer controlling us. We have learned (or are still learning) how to react to things soberly, and not addictively. We stop and think or consider, instead of immediately reaching for a bottle. We accept responsibility for our actions and become accountable for them. We are emotionally mature.

We do mourn it, in a fashion during our Fourteenth Station. We do not wish to relive it or resurrect it, as it were. We instead mourn the lost opportunities and the people missing from our lives that would still be in them had we not taken that drink.

But we do not dwell on it. What was our life before sobriety is now over and done. There is no going back and undoing things. For whatever reason we abused alcohol, and the reasons for it, may for our purposes, remain a mystery. We were alcoholics, but now we are sober, and we have learned via a very sorrowful and rough road the tools and things we need to keep sober.

The Church is always there to receive us and to patch us back up when time are tough. Through Mass and the Sacraments we are sustained and kept alive in the Spirit.

We are sober, and we are now resurrected through Christ!

About the Author

Paul Sofranko sobered up on May 22, 2002. Afterwards, he decided that while a 12 Step Program may be effective and very useful for some, he needed something more. Therefore he explored the religion of his childhood and returned to the Catholic Church, from which he had been away for nearly 15 years. He's been happy with his decision ever since.

Connect with Me Online:

I blog at:

www.SoberCatholic.com

About the Photographer

Rose Sofranko is happily married to this book's author, and is also an artist and photographer.

Her portfolio may be found at:

www.Artist4God.net

Made in the USA
San Bernardino, CA
28 August 2016